ROGUELIKE

Also by Mathew Henderson

The Lease

ROGUELIKE

poems

Mathew Henderson

ANANSI

Published in Canada in 2020 and the USA in 2020 by House of Anansi Press Inc.
www.houseofanansi.com

House of Anansi Press is committed to protecting our natural environment. As part of our efforts, the interior of this book is printed on paper that is made from second-growth forests and is acid-free.

24 23 22 21 20 1 2 3 4 5

Library and Archives Canada Cataloguing in Publication

Title: Roguelike / Mathew Henderson
Names: Henderson, Mathew, 1985– author.
Description: Poems.
Identifiers: Canadiana (print) 2019017238X I Canadiana (ebook) 20190172398 I
ISBN 9781487007812 (softcover) I ISBN 9781487007829 (hardcover) I
ISBN 9781487007836 (PDF)
Classification: LCC PS8615.E525 R64 2020 I DDC C811/.6—dc23

Cover design: Alysia Shewchuk

We acknowledge for their financial support of our publishing program the Canada Council for the Arts, the Ontario Arts Council, and the Government of Canada.

Printed and bound in Canada

For Mary, who loves like no one else.

EARLY/GAME

***

FISHING, FEBRUARY, 1993

She worked a boat in Louisiana.
Let the shit that comes up in a handful
of prawns dye the marriage from her
hands, thatched her shoulders
with muscle until her half-bare back
blended her with the row of boys
as they spat and bent and straightened.

But how far is that? Aren't prawns
just lobsters? Isn't every boy me?
Didn't she remember when I found
her hiding in my room? Could she
not tell then that she'd never be like
anything that could be so much like me?

AFTER THE ARCTIC, APRIL, 1993

You played Donkey Kong Country from the top bunk
in the girls' room, as they watched from blankets
below. But your mother saw only glaciers, and long
after you fell asleep, she lay crossways on the bed,
awake with an ear to your sisters, willing their breath
to sync, bodies to fall into each other, into her,
to prove that there is only one child for each of us,
that an ocean poured into glasses remains a single thing.
And even as their eyelids were about to flit as one,
she saw you catching her awake, your face in the black
television, her so near to tundra, ready to run again.

LEAVING WOOLFE'S CORNER

The last to leave, she wiped prints from the walls,
bleached your nosebleed from the sink. Left nothing
of herself for them to read, no cells or skin to roll
over slides and under scopes like little rodent bones.

When she disappeared for good, you sat alone
in the bungalow, put the absence on her restless nature,
even as she rushed downriver, dragging her scent
and broken wing, pulling the foxes from you.

Had she told you everything, you would have said
you had no fear of trench-coat men, but of how dark
her room could be, how she was felt seeping past
the hinges, how you'd piss outside to keep from near
her door. You knew already how a house could pile
upon your chest, could pin you sure as a railway spike.

AND SHE WORE THE GREAT COAT OF A BOAR

In those weeks before, Talos had cursed them
with wilted skins, tusks that grew strange
and long in their mouths. And still they fell on,
unstoppable across the field, young mouths
sewn against hunger and old meat. At herd's
centre, your mother crawls hidden beneath
a great, grey skin, dragging her cheeks along
the earth. She hums the story again (shit scent)
and again, two of your brightest buttons, again,
pinned, again, to the leather they dart like eyes.

BORN UPRIGHT

A bird or mouse or pet, the secret
in killing is that you can't, but do —
a man, a wyrm — and you've snapped
the necks of birds and fish in your hands.
You could do the same to her father,
if it was him. A man is like a bird;
you wake up clenched, your fists wet.
You betray your mothers. All mothers.
The quiet mother alive within yourself.
As if you could ever forget her story.

SHE WAS ONCE A LONE AND WILD MOUTH

Between the yards, she gripped Lori's forearm
and hair in her hands like those last youthful
days when she tanned without sunscreen.
Her gums bled against her dentures, her wrist
bruised from you pulling her back. The neighbour's
blood, stray lipstick on her teeth. She called out
for Catherine, for Sheryl and Katrina. Couldn't she
see you were sisters too? The iron was intoxicating;
you'd soon bite yourself in the shower. Didn't she
see that no distance could come between you?
Spread thin enough you can reach across anything.

LATENCY

You were born like a knife. Like blood
cells thirty years late, her body's immunity
patty-caking up a golem with nothing
left to kill. She should've mudded herself
up another mother, planned for bad ping
because now you're here and angry
with no one to smack. Every eye you
poke is monocled, is glass or floats
in too-thick goop. Even today, you're
a mad dog, not waiting for the urge,
but for permission, for the slack leash
and the way skin folds against tooth.
You trace your run up a leg like pantyhose.

LIMINAL

There are those nights in the city after work when I find my way
free of the usual currents, get caught in another eddy and wind up
outside of it all. The traveller's dilemma: to arrive, in seconds,
apart from what you were, the passenger in the aisle as the plane
reaches that height at which it's no longer possible you were just
there, just one of the people, all your stone-solid intention less
than a tree or barn or network of fences. Does this moment
wait in everything? If we twist hard enough, won't we find
the flat cardboard of our bones visible; why can we not escape?
I want to fall through the world, stick my full height in a space
too small and stand anyway, be forced down, through the arena
and fall and keep falling. This, I think, is what you've wanted too.
Though I won't speak to you, I'd hold your hand at the tree-lined
peak above the water, and we could count in nods, go on three,
fall fast and hard and true enough to land with a little perspective.

YOUR FATHER SLEEPING OFF THE NIGHT-SHIFT

In your bed for the first eight hours of every day.
You'd also find him drinking tea, humming, watching
the toilet flush. He'd await you in the woods, the kitchen.
Emerge from the slick of mushroom behind your boot,
fall from the flat of a knife. Rushing back to your bedroom
door, you'd find him, a winter bear, snoring, permanent.
He coughed sleeptalk, a voice rumbling from your stomach,
his mind to yours, his thoughts to yours. You know your room,
you think, the navy walls. But just as you've never known
the man, only the father of him, you can't recall the walls
in the rest of the house. You carry in your mind a navy room,
littered toys, a sleeping man. When he shifts from stomach
to side, you lose balance and weight. You beg him to wake up.

PICNICS

She called my older sister and said she'd kill herself at a picnic table
with little rec-centre sandwiches, gorge herself to death. *Soon*, she said.
She called my father and told him she'd bathe until her skin sloughed
from her frame. To Karen, she wrote about lying on the forest floor,
swore she wouldn't move until mushrooms grew from her heart.
She always smelled my rot. Was I not called? Did she wash my skin
in baby soap to start? Did she draw a sponge gently along my neck?
When that old-fruit scent lingered in my sweat, my skin and breath,
the Irish Spring? The bleach? Did she imagine steel wool on my back
until I finally came clean? Until my insides awoke, and I grew to be
a man who could answer his phone, who'd rush past guards and flip
a picnic table, throw old cheese sandwiches at the gulls. Who'd fall
on my ass trying to stomp that stupid hospital gown into the ground.

GHOST CAR

I see my father still, walking about my house
in outline, the pace ghost I can't disable. Funny
it's him and not you. If you had been my father
too, would you be shading ahead of me each year?
Where was Mary, my dad, when she was thirty?
Thirty-two? When did she buy her house? My teeth
are fine — my father didn't have a brush until she was
fourteen. My calves would seem enormous landing
in your footprints. I strive to meet your standard,
your manly frame, how you fed the ones you loved.

THE WAY YOU REMEMBER IT

Her father was a drunk, you think, but you
remember nothing of her mother. She said
she'd been a girl when they died, but she was
younger, an infant, her hair static with promise.
You want to make her an athlete, whisked
away on scholarship, but that's just to skip
the violence: the scientists nearly pulling her
little arm from its body. Or was that her father,
yanking on limbs like stubborn joints of meat?

But, no — he's dead. You can see her afloat
in the tank of liquid, tubes in her like pins.
You feel her rage retreat as the needle hits
her neck. They sucked lightning from her
bones and watched from behind the barricades
as she lit bulbs, then buildings, brought rats
screeching back to life. To draw her spark,
they'd welt the pointless flesh on the backs
of her legs and arms, striking down with sticks.

Or was that also her father? A star pupil, she went
empty as predicted, her face falling away from
purpose like leaves. To be certain she was done
with screaming, they brought her to the homestead,
where she did not cry or run, where they locked
her in the shower, where they tossed her food
under the bed. She did everything in twice-a-days

with a doctor watching. Or was that her father,
her brother, a man she met while skipping school?

THE MONTH OF YOUR BIRTH

I am told that I was born in the month
when the sea retreated from the shores,
that when the oldest father walked across
the flats, he returned dripping salts,
and claimed the water hungered for a son.
The youngest who could bear a child,
unmarried, they sent her to the forest,
alone, and she wept and made me.
She took us to where the ocean had been.
But the water did not know her anger,
and it boiled and raged when it rushed us,
razing the village, crushing the walls.

She was cast out, and you are told this
is when she learned to hate herself.
They say your first memory must always
be of her greed. You keep an earlier image:
a woman speaking to herself in the wood,
her blade over the last memory of a canoe.

TAXONOMY

The Southern Colorado Hare is a lie.
Like the cake, it's a promise, a try-on!
Rabbits don't mate in the same place
they were born, don't die nestled
in the bones of their mothers or sons;
that's only something I said to keep
from saying we're stuck, year over year,
in that same clearing in the woods,
another lie. Look, there's no great herd
of hares forming circles in the forest.
I didn't pull myself from the roots
of their boneyard up onto my mother's
back, haven't clung that same way
to the necks of the women I've loved.
It's a joke! C'mon. It's just kidding.
Don't be like that. I know you wanted
to talk. Go ahead, tell me again how sad
you get. How it smothers you every few
months like it did your mother. Your heart
gasps under eczema. You find her housecoat
and wear it to bed, wear it to piss, wear it
to the corner store for Coke cans and candy.
Tell me about it again. Another fucking time.
You think it's just you who's caught in the loop?
She's not dead. She's out there too, caking,
making hares. She's gathered you up from owl
pellets! She's not high and sad, sick in a Walmart

parking lot, in her little orange car, the battery
dying and the last heat of her Timmies going
cold in her hands. It's boring. It's just talk.
Don't think about it. Have I ever told you
about the Southern Colorado Hare? Try-on!

THE GRIND

***

THE KONAMI CODE

Was it a Dark Souls note that told me how to tap
the ups and downs and ups and downs against
my thigh until my thigh began to tap them back?
Or was it Jessica, who loved me, who taught me
to unclasp my heart, so it would not fly away but sit,
bent-winged and beating b, a, b, a? Who read Salinger
as I slept until the Glass kids appeared in my dreams,
stood beside my father on the Hillsborough Bridge
in his thirties, when he talked a woman out of jumping?
Was it when Franny turned at the edge of the bridge,
The NPCs are dying! And my dad, who had never saved
anyone in his life, grabbed me at the back of my neck,
said *We're all dying, boy!* My sister says that for years
she's surfaced after every dive in the closet of my room
in Horton Park just after my first panic attack left me limp
on the floor. Even now, after a swim, she drips over
to my body and presses her fingers left-right-left-right
into my sternum, like she could maybe bruise me
well and young enough to seed the sequence.
Like by now, I might wake to find a life unlocked.

ROGUELIKE

We first put faith in the loudest and brightest, in those things
that constantly reassert their own existence. I found a faith
in your voice: a sun of sound. I bathed in it until I peeled.
I believed in the strict cord of your arm, that tight, wicker strength.

They speak of you in the Caves of Qud, the tortoise and crab,
the glowfish. The Great Saltback kneels, says you travel in my grin.
In Joppa, you glowed, ate watervine and planned a pilgrimage.
In Kyakukya Village, you supped with an albino ape. You will smell
of smoked mushrooms for months, and I am just weeks behind you.

Yours was a hungry faith. An out-of-doors, uncloistered faith.
It may please you to know that my prodigy in this has not faded.
You taught a hyperventilating faith, an IRL faith, a panicked faith,
a faith with follow-through just less than 30%. I once placed
faith in the efficacy of my desires, in the potency of my intent.

The Great Saltback grins, says you travel in my kneel,
in the prayers I still queue nightly in your name,
tickets torn by the deli counter. I wish you'd started a map.
I wish that when the Barathrumites begged you to stay,
you'd stayed. They still howl when they recall your jokes.
They smile, fondly, terrifyingly, at your hairless cheeks.

Intent, I've learned, is impotent. Desire is what we do
when we do nothing. Did you learn this too? Like everything,
it nearly killed me. I'm fragile. There's that song, how's it go?

Don't worry, you can still kill yourself. Did you love that tune
when you were younger? Is it something one grows out of?
I learned all of this long after our last scene together.

They say that when you travel, you should like, see the real Qud,
see the Qud you can't see online. You need a local guide, they say,
to see the local scene, but all I've got is you, and your build is shit.
Did you hire local? Travel with a caravan? I think you rolled blind.
If I had come first, I wouldn't learn to love it here; it wouldn't stick.

The first time I wanted to re-roll, I was six. The squirrels descended
on the orchard like locusts, in a soft-fur, sharp-tooth flood you could
wade in. I felt their legs catching in my throat. I noped the fuck home
before I choked for good, but kept playing — sunk costs; 240,000 hours
ago. Now I see this world seed sucks: too RNG heavy, too pay-to-win.

In the deepest part of Qud, in the jungle under the caves under
the jungle, my father sits with my sisters and a stuffed duck,
wishing more and more into existence. His syntax is failing him.
He wishes for a [Young Mary] and a Jilted Lover pierces his shoes.
[Once Wife] and his feet turn to iron. My ego is off the charts.
I have torn my skirts in the pits of Golgotha, chosen survival over
friendship. I'm still looking for you. Ajencir, the great fly, promises
I'll find you in the Eater's Glade. You covet the secrets told about you.

WHEN THEY WOULD HUNT

Before there was hawk, there would be a shadow
hawking overhead, and before there was crow,
there would be a darkness, crowing in the limbs.

She and my father wiped asses at the group home.
When she set out the trash, the crows tore her body
to pieces, and the pills hummed in their cups.

But none were as hungry as my mother. She rode
him through the undergrowth, her scrape across
a door. The lolling head, horns along the wallpaper.

In the dust under the beds, the patients traced
their murals: a child become a hound, a man become
a bear. She inhales, and I smell the salt of her skin.

Her tongue flicks, and my closet fills with casserole.
She stalks my early years, hunts my life, her nose
to the ground of my teens. The last time we speak

before she dies, a hum and crow in the distance,
a bear at the edge of my sight. She dashes her skull
on the wall, and from the crack, a hawk takes flight.

RIP

Eventually, she'll R.I.P. all this shit. RIP the drugs,
RIP the kids, rip the Lysol and bleach that sting.
Rip the way you memorized the angle for every
jump in every level in the game. Rip the hole
in the wall of stage three, the warp to stage five.
Rip the hole in your bedroom closet, the hole
behind the dummy foreground, the one that
grows a tunnel to your twenties. Rip your twenties,
rip nostalgia, fuck your thirties, your adolescence,
all your pills and plastic toys. Rip the glitch
that turns our toons to text. Rip this run. Reset.

DIABLO II

Your mother belting Tupac on a highway in Buttfuck,
Saskatchewan, waiting for the pixels to part, the sky
to spill the futures of her children all over the hood,
their lives rolling through the potato field. Dig in,
do better, move up, marry, divorce, move on. Pack it
all in U-Boxes, take the risks, bet on yourself, bet
on success! Just know you'll never look up to see
the white of your lover's eyes spread from their sockets,
envelope her face. Reach 1200% mf, and you still
won't find magic. Know that there will be no light
behind your skin either, no galaxies that starprick out
of the holes her nails go to dig. You can fuck or drive,
punch and win forever. You still won't find a glitch,
not a single drop that hasn't been dropped before.

POLLY

There was that dog you had in Alberta, the Pomeranian, American
Eskimo thing, and the kitten dad shot. Or that run-away-and-come-
back-with-one-eye cat, the one we closed the door on, the one we
secretly fed outside and stepped around or over, to save pant legs
from the blood. You know how I think on animals, but that dog, I
forget its name. Terri bought it for you early, before that friendship
died like all ours do, yours like a full Lego starship against the wall
and mine like wet cornstarch going loose again in the bowl. But that
dog got itself crushed while I was back at school. I was glad to be
away for that. Glad to skip the crying, all your fucking wailing, to not
have to care by proxy. I told you it was stupid, but you got attached.
You loved it even as it bolted for the door. Oh, damn. You weren't
supposed to know about the kitten. Maybe I gave him up. It's not so
odd to end like that back home; I've had to handle a couple cats
myself. Sometimes, they just get too hurt. How could you be so
careless, to love such a stupid little thing? Such a pointless
animal? Didn't you already see the way I'd hurt people to hurt
people, how my skin rolled at the corner of your sight, like
headlights over houses in the dark?

IN MIDGAR

Had you resigned yourself to what you were
in the beginning, your father would be young,
bailing water as he paddled. They'd hire babysitters
and drink into the night. But you accepted nothing.

Anyway, what would you do? School parking lot,
three o'clock, out behind the gym? Maybe you
and some cousins could drag Sephiroth by his hair
out behind the rink and kick his guts like guys
would have done back in the day, and if he looks
at her again, you all find him after class and tie
him to a post and golf-club his knees.
Jenova would start wearing her slippers
to the grocery store and the moms would shun her.
Show some class, Jenova! Your people have always
gone protecting while the women get together
and say out loud, *I understand, yes, I know, nothing,*
no, none of it should ever be this way again.

Yet, you grew. You ended a hundred stories
and reread your own. But if you had quit
at the prologue, she'd have gentle brown hair,
her skin made of petals, you'd be forever
an infant — or just dead within your crib.
And the dead would remain the dead. No elixir for it.
No old-clock secrets. You should never
have journeyed to the caves, never escaped

the city, but held the flower girl in sector
seven, hid your eyes, let Midgar burn.

PRINCESS MONONOKE

Long after Ashitaka was first touched by a demon,
after the boars began their rampage, I found it playing
on freemium channels. As a child, I'd dreamt a saucer
ripped through the air above my house. Chest aching,
breath fast and empty. As the lepers began to sing,
the room became bright as an operating table —
less a lighting than a purging. Like Dyson himself had sucked
the shadows from the room. I saw each spore of pollen
shed by a thrown pair of slippers, saw them worn outside,
smoke and wet dandelions. There's no safety in possibility,
promise panics. You came home to find me hyperventilating,
my hands on the coffee table. You were sure I fell asleep,
awoke mid-dream, confused. But I remember your knowing,
your fear. How you held me like we hold the things we lose.
When Eboshi kills the forest spirit, her hands creak and crack,
your grandmother's ring can be heard, a tap against the wood.

QUESTING

At the town gate, face north and blow this whistle.
Bring me the fins of fourteen salmon, the bills of four
black ducks and you will never again gasp for air.
Kill a hundred town guardsmen, plant their banners
in the jarl's armoury, inspire the town to rise up —
this is how we do good, throwing force like wet socks
against the wall. Get stripped and return your clothes
to their original owners, leave the waiter's notes
in the pantry, take credit, fuck the maid — sorry,
seduce the servant. Arrive in time to move your hand
over a bowl of virgin scuttle milk as the second moon
eclipses the first. Remember my questions in order.
Disguise yourself as a man of god, a child of god,
the child of a god, a child god. I need nine gizzards
from birds of prey. Collect the quilt from the tower
where I was raised, the blanket my mother crocheted
for me, before my older and after my younger sister's,
blue and grey and coffee-stained like her dentures.
Collect the hooks she used, the reason she started.

VANA'DIEL

Raix wears what you tell him to, /sits
or /follows as the Nyquil, Bentylol,
and caffeine give you flashes of a man
over your shoulder, glitching about
the basement, screeching like packing tape.
Your neck weakens; your hand flattens over
the mouse. You flash back to standing between
your mother and the pills, watching her wobble
in her chair. But your neck or grip fails.
Your forehead opens against the edge
of the desk. You come to on your back,
face sticky, feet raw from the space heater,
and Raix looks down from your monitor.
Arms outstretched, he praises the sun.

AUNT HAZELWOOD

How are you going to calm the winds on the mountain peak
or smooth the waters of the inner lake? I don't know, really.
I could call you right now and talk it out though. I imagine
being onstage and your cousin standing and telling me
how I'm wrong, the great abandoner. I answer so well,
composed, compassionate. I return to an airport hotel.
In the bathroom, I reddit. I press a safety pin into my thigh.

FROG'S THEME

I'd leave the game idle, turn the TV all the way up.
You'd fill the entire rest of the house, cleaning,
your Annie Lennox joining my Mitsuda, the two
of them telling the countryside there would be
no more I-love-yous. The language, there are days
when it really does start leaving me, the internal one,
the machine bits, scrappy bits that connect circuits
and chips more than the parts that make a program run,
the parts that make sure apples fall and birds fly,
make creatures mate and age and die. Not the bits
that turn the sunset that shade of pink that sets us
calling friends to the same window for the same
sunset. It's the deep parts that go missing,
turn German. Glenn became a blur of grey-brown
pixels for a week, and I still loved him. I loved him,
and when I walk into a room with Annie Lennox,
I see you scrubbing kitchen cabinets, wonder how,
even at nine, I failed to see your grace, to study you,
learn how to suck every last feeling from the song.

LUCCA'S MOTHER

Talk to her a million times and she says the same thing,
until Lucca sneaks away, sneaks back like it were her secret
to hide, as if it were a thing to be set right, like fixing her legs
is the same as loving her. L, A, R, A, I fucked up the input.
Love, apparently, is just what you do, and everything we do
has rules. But my mother, you can be sure, would wheel us
to the fair for the races at least some of the time. And I still
steal away from campfires, tap my knuckles against loose bark,
and listen. Imagine a side-quest that makes it easier to love.

CONFLICT RESOLUTION

Someday we won't remember this,
our lives like homebrew campaigns,
bundled sprites and shader packs
by some designer who's just as worried
as we are that she's losing her art,
just as scared the office is where she'll die.
I'm off track. My face is stretched around
the ball from Babes in Inktown Pinball.
I can't slow down without opening my mouth.
There are some geniuses out there still,
finding new ways to vanish/x-zone, to build
themselves strange. But I'm not one of them.
It doesn't take a genius to tell you to max
your agility. It's a basic build, but I'm so fast,
I can kite mobs forever, dodge problems
before I even know they're real.

CRONO

I.

I've heard that when you heard, you could be heard cursing me.
You didn't see the body, but I heard you were seen writing notes
like math class to tie to their legs, the birds you'd send fluttering
like unread flags through a mail server. I've heard that you never
stopped pulling back the curtains, you keep asking me awake.

II.

My father was on the water when your goose dove at
him with word of me. He already knew, the bit of him
I carried having rushed back a week earlier, nailing
his chest as he stepped from the shower, drying his
shoulders with the slap of it. Did you think of the day
I was born, how you handed me back and forth like
a breathing tube, or maybe of how, even near the end,
hating each other for real, you could still sometimes
lie quiet against his chest? Perhaps, like me, he cried
only in his room, against a stomach. (I cry loudly now,
real *uh-huh uh-huh* stuff. I say, relax, it's good for you)
He packed a bag. Too many socks. Kit Kats. Smokes.

III.

When she was small, Jessica wore a crown and flight
goggles like a prince. Warm words in a cold tone, a gaze
she slashed around the room like a knife. She had just
boarded the second bus, the last of the week. Not until
Kipling did she notice the wren on her bag, your note.
She read it twice, showed it to her mother, her sister,
therapist, friend, other friend, stranger, rabbi, and yogi.

IV.

Pulling on track pants, Rockon set his mind to cereal.
He had woken with a bird on his chest, a note. He ate,
showered, instagrammed the duck. He once asked me
if I had ever been in love, but he would never ask that,
putting only the material to the material, grouping things
as he does. He asked if I'd ever had that Russian soup
that's cold, and would I like to? But she'd ask you anything.
Jessica: *Do you take anti-depressants? Something I can*
get you? You think you'd ever like me to fuck your ass?
When they first met, he asked if she was travelling far.
Yes, I knew him too, he spoke of you, did you ever love
him, would you ever walk behind him as he washed dishes,
press your mouth between his shoulder blades, as I have?
He told her it was a beautiful day coming, and was she
going where he was? They held hands, and when bandits
came upon them in the night, they joined at the mouth.
When they sang, bandits lost limbs like hard-shaken dolls.

V.

Tessa, long dead, was the first, the bird landing nearby,
her hip still shattered but numb, and she smelled you
on the note, snapped at the bird, ate it whole. She pulled
herself up, and started off, the raven asleep inside her.
Her teeth could get a man's neck as well as a goose wing,
haul an ex by the arm as gently as food from your hands.
She can't sleep without the snow of a television nearby.

VI.

Anna was in love and angry, writing, flashing in and out
of time. She took her notebook, nine of my favourite words,
and the bird you sent. Tessa took to her quicker than I did.
But she won me too. Every time you looked at her, a shift
from focus, an aberration in the eye, a floater curling away.
When we first kissed, I feared I'd open my eyes and find
I'd been falling, eaten whole. She remained dangerous,
the calm and gentle of her like back-floating in the Atlantic.
It was a fear that slows the heart, the ocean with all its salt
in the settle of her stomach at the small of my back.

VII.

Tessa, half covered in leaves, fur bloodmatted, found Anna
asleep at the New Brunswick border, lapped at the dust
in her eyes. And she pants, smiles. A touch near the neck,
a rub, a belly scratch. Anna pressed their foreheads together,
stared eye to eye. This is a good dog. This is the dog for her.
She uses an edged rock to open the top of the dog's back
and chews sticks and scarf to rub into the cracked hips.
A kiss on the nose! Pats on ass, a run in leaves. You cute!

VIII.

Simon, the brother, the giant non-son, fell asleep
two years before I died. He woke to a bird's beak on his
eyelid, our smell, you, me, and the pit behind our house.
He shuffled up to his height, his feet big as Buicks. He'd
eat the bird at the end, he promised. Until then, it circled,
cawing out the names of everyone we knew together,
even barely, of Greg, Super, his whole dead family.

IX.

Dogs are big right now, having a moment overnight,
so Tessa, with her cool, ghost-girl fur and grin is a born fit,
a leader, a quester, furious. And how will things shake out
when she sees my father once again? Will he tell her how
he almost hit the guy who clipped her? How he'd almost
brought my sister that night? Will Tessa nuzzle him to say,
in dog, *It's okay and always was*, and *of course, of course.*

X.

A few of you, still smokers, sat smoking, and you started
telling them all about the gas station attendant who tried
to charge you for premium when you were sure, you were
sure, you'd selected regular, but the manager, he sorted
things out in the end. How could he not, it was clear who
had been right, you said, welling up. And Simon came over
and rubbed your shoulders, and Dad started whittling down
a branch like I'd done as a kid, a little wooden knife falling
from his blade, and Jessica, who had joined you after a few
drinks, laughed and laughed at every beat in your story,
how you even did the voices, and you started really crying
then, to be so loved. You cried and cried and you told
Simon he'd always been an arrogant little fucker, and you told
my father I'd be alive if he'd been a real father, if he'd taught
me to fly-fish. And you told Jessica she was your truest friend,
that you'd never betray her. You bought her coat hangers
from the dollar store. Ribboned in red, the holidays came.

XI.

A friend once told me that he first heard his call to medicine
on your dealer's examination table. That an addict, your doctor,
taught him the dignity of healing, the joy of service. But it's not
him you're waiting for with the party piled on matching beds
in the Moncton Airport Hotel. You're waiting for the man who
cut you open, and pulled me across the threshold. Simon slept
in a slump like piled coats at a party. Dad didn't yell or call you crazy.
He cooed to your pigeons, petted their heads. The doctor a bulb,
shining white in grey rags. He was so bright everything else went
dark, turned the room halfway to nothing, shut down the *Pawn
Stars* rerun Rockon had been playing, and all your scars began to ache.
Guru of time. You offered to open yourself again, pulled a blade
from Jessica's belt and gestured, but he promised that it wouldn't
work. Some spells you get to use just once. Some words run out.

XII.

Instead, he tells you a story. When you were a younger woman,
and the house was at its worst, I ran the pit behind our property.
At first, I ran alone, but then the hints began: a tangle of hair
from behind the branches, the smell of person piss in my forts.
Once as I ran fully over rabbit hill, I tripped, landing right on him.
In all our struggling to break free, we wrapped ourselves together,
tangled our coat strings and curls, and when we finally stood apart,
we saw our faces, same selves staring, our slow walk and touching
cheeks, our lips flaking and rough until wet. He held me, my twin,
he tried. His hands pressing on my abdomen. Pine needles, stubble,
sharp in mouth, on my neck, nearly sweet. He was the impossible
place, the curve in the tallest branch. One night, I hit him behind
the ear with the sharp end of a shovel, buried him blinking under
that tree where we saw the coyote, Simon and I. You'll use him.
I did. Now that they know the story, the party feels his presence.
Distracting, soft, a fly on the arm, a lover's eyelid at the neck.

XIII.

While Jessica went looking for the body with Dad and Simon,
the rest of you waited at the hotel. An hour on foot after a full
morning's drive. At the pit, they ate cucumber sandwiches
and listened for the homunculus blinking underground.
They barely needed shovels. They found him backhoed into
the side of a sheer wall, his hand hanging out of the red dirt,
a blown seed on the furrow. What a shit garden I'd planted.
For years I blamed my own spare harvest on the soil conditions,
climate change, maybe you. But I planted that boy in good dirt,
wet earth with a lot to give, and he blinked away the years.
Jessica looked at him and saw what I once saw, a plot of land,
an acreage she could retire to. Blink. Blink. Simon carried it.
My father, the collector, tied a broken shovel to his back,
and Jessica found the spool of Gaspar thread. She tugged,
and felt the doctor tugging back, but harder, and from inside.

XIV.

Anna with the temporal eggs inside her stomach pushes fingers
at her abdomen like a doctor and Simon hums and hums
and the two of them are sure this one is whole. I worry too
that you're all about to use him as the vessel, that you'll
gather on the peak and you'll all hold him down, eight
hands grasping, while Tessa tears his throat and lets him
leak to empty, like we are crabs, and I, having grown too
large for my shell, could slip just as easily into his. This isn't
it though, is it? I'm getting carried away. You would read this
and love it. You'd miss a lot, but love it like you've always
loved, a quilt over a model town, touching every street,
toppling the houses with your stray sway and tug.

XV.

I guess I'm hoping for this twist ending, where I've been you
the whole time, letting the ravens loose, bringing the doctor
and leading everyone to the place where the world is an eyelid,
and it's this big reveal, and if you look back the voice will
match, will say, *Sort of, look, it makes sense now, right?* I was
speaking from this position the whole time, and what
do you think *that's* all about? Here's my take: I said before
that I was worried no one would ever do this for me, would
send themselves unsafe into the ether or would want to,
but that's all of us isn't it? And you can be unloved and fine.
A tragic self is an acceptable self. You can make that work.
What about a selfish self, a cold self, someone who would *not*,
for anyone, mother or friend, make that journey in the real
world. That's who I'm afraid of. There are good victims
and heroes and failures but there are no good bystanders,
no good monsters. The good bystander becomes involved,
right? If they don't, they lack goodness or they lack ability,
and a good one without means is just another kind of victim.

XVI.

I wasn't sure how I died, if I was hit by a truck or thinned out
in a hospital room or if my heart exploded early from caffeine,
Adderall, and an inability to control anything at all. It's clearer
now, this far along, that I let my wrists bleed out over the side
of the tub. Isn't that a twist? It shouldn't be! 87% of men kill
themselves by age eighteen; 87% of them stay dead too. Men don't
kid around, nosir. Maybe you saw this years ago, driving across
the prairie. Maybe you really found a bug, maybe the sky opened
up and showed your only son slipping under dark red bathwater.
Is that what's made you mad all these years? Was it never about
the toast crumbs in the butter? Exactly what sort of miracle
are you going for here? I hated that Crono never got a choice.
Is that why I quit the side-quests? Did I know as a boy to let
some things be? When did I forget that? I tried for a month
to die a good death, to swap spots with a lady who steps
in front of a bus, or a stranger getting hurt. It doesn't happen;
ladies know about buses, and I'm scared to talk to strangers.
Some gift. You fuckers. I'm sure. You can't bring me here in a rage
like this with nowhere to set it down, nothing to kill, teach me
about better natures when all I want is to wrong every scene,
to stand over you in pieces and feel unrightable, to know that one
thing worked, is final, won't go back, won't repeat. I've ended
something. I killed myself for sure. Cast, but don't you set
your hook in my cheek and pull, or when I open my mouth
to gasp that first real breath, I swear, I'll close it on your throat.

XVII.

After you showed me the Bible, I started nightly prayers,
felt God as a hole in the centre of my bed, a promise of more.
I've felt it since, with Anna or Jessica on my back, in how quiet
Rockon and I could be, the way Simon and I would wander
the street, making and unmaking everything. How dad showed
me the string on the fly, how I learned to seek the string in all
things, and how Tessa never turned me away, not even once.
You were the only person who seemed as rightly terrified as me.
These are the thinnest places I've been, the only places I've
been where I can imagine finding a seam, I think, or an edge,
or a wall of Jell-O with some give. Or, shit as it was, some nights,
the air by the well, the sky, it all seemed alive, like the animal
scatter in the distance was less a part of the painting and more
a scrape on the frame. There are so many endings for us, Mary,
but it always starts the same. The sudden light, the sleepy gulls.

END/GAME

***

STREETCAR HEATMAP

I was going to my dentist or doctor in the neighbourhood where I'd spent several years in love, and I began to see myself on the street. I watched myself falling into every seat on the streetcar like I'd done coming home, sitting sideways or facing forward, with long hair or short or wearing the jacket I liked, or sweating through my shirt. The car was crowded with me. And I filled the street. From the window I saw a memory of myself in a store I'd never entered, I saw that I had lived with a tension in my hands, cracking my knuckles against how much everything seemed to matter. The heatmap of it would turn the city red. I'd flash back to life, rushing right, shooting from the ledge, choosing left or right as if I weren't caught up in the same rabid inertia as everyone else, as if I could step from the current that set me waking and going to work and checking my ass pocket for my wallet and kissing goodnight and fucking or not and all the thousands of loves and millions of silences, and the desperate promise that I wanted to work and love, go west. As if the great map above me could never capture me in thin red lines.

NEWDIVES

They wake upright, no gasps, intubated, salty water draining from
their eyelids to their feet. Practice keeps their hands from pulling at
the tube even before they remember who they are, that they are not
us. Not anymore. His drinks coffee in the mess hall, watered down.
White cotton and loafers. Yours comes walking up and sits, and *We
can't talk about it* mine says, dropping corn from his spoon. *But
how?* she asks. *It was thirty years, Mathew.* Silence. Another time,
he woke holding himself at the waist, having broken the straps
around his wrists, having broken the straps around his arms, having
broken the straps around his shoulders, having broken the strap
around his waist. When it's cold, he can't feel his little finger where I
was cut by hot glass in the bonfire, at three. He feels the safety pin
in my thigh at seventeen. Have you tried to conceive of yourself as a
fluid? Have you thought to touch the flowing river of minds? Have
you allowed yourself to join it, to settle into them, to find balance
in dilution?

SEVERANCE

I am Thing T. Thing. The hand in the halls.

Once, I was a body, too monstrous a body,

I rose from the bottom of a box,

only to light cigars and point and sign *Okay!*

But I think I might have dreamt that body, if hands dream.

The mind is what the brain does. Clever, the brain

is the body. The mind is what the body does.

I am Thing T. Thing. My fingerpads hurt like a cat

after it's declawed. You see how I yell in my nails?

I am the body, the mind the hand does.

What should a mind of hands fear?

Does it write *frightened* across the gamepad?

Do the buttons sing a song for other hands to hear?

Let me out let me out this is not a dance.

I'm dying. A pins-and-needles hand,

a hand held under an ass cheek. I'm pricks

on fingertips. Asleep at the dog-eared end

of the last chapter of *The Wheel of Time.*

I am the hand the sin does. If the body sins,

it can be severed. If the mind sins, send the sin away.

Sever the body. Sever a body. Make two.

MY OTHER SISTER

I'm sure you think of her more often than I do,
my thoughts drifting there every three months
or so, like she's another degree or a hiking trip.
Surely, it's more often for you, dwelling as you do,
raging like we do at all that's lost to us, past
knowing or control. Often, I think I might be near
her, like today, like now. With the way this woman
beside me on the plane looks like you if you had
grown old loved, if my father had known how
to be more to you. Her face, mom, is just like
yours, I swear. I started counting your sisters
before your daughters, but it might also be that
I'm on my way to PEI, to visit the place you were
sent, hidden and tucked away. Where you prayed,
of course, and wished to die, and sweated, puked,
but also where I went to school, years earlier,
where I watched *Fantasia* at the top of the attic
stairs, and where years before that, nuns had run
an orphanage. And if I followed her, my sister,
mother, whoever she is, I'd tell her son to visit you
at the hospital, the psych ward, treatment centre.
I'd make him ask her for the whole of her story
in cursive, in CSV, digitally signed, in triplicate, stamped.

RETRO-HEROICS

Now, when I sit on the streetcar and a man at the back
of the train raises his voice above his head like a mallet,
screaming or glaring or hitting himself, I remember that
I was born for this, the hard point of my elbow perfect for his
head. I keep my eyes down, count the imaginary lines
as he crosses them. It won't be heroic, I decide, if you hit
him when he's down, so get him while he's still falling.
A lot of men become victims because they back off too soon.
That's what I've heard. It could have been as simple
when my mom got sick, but a woman has to hit you three
times, so I ate my elbows whole, and when I could only
lick them, I bit chunks from my shoulder, and when they
would not digest, I sobbed for hours in the washroom.
I kept hunching, even when they rubbed my back,
even after the cramps. I howled, I bruised my legs until
you couldn't read the quit in them. And I still know not
to back off too quick, I know to push. I was made for this.

SEVERANCE II

Us or where we live, the man or the home,
the person with the child inside them?
Is it the pieces coming together,
or just the knitted atoms, touching?
And then, are you and I a body?
Are we a body with everything?
And if I leave you, as I have, am I alone
or severed? If a limb lives on without its body,
is it a body still? If we're the things within
the body, do you become me if I chew your skin,
do I become the you in your body
if you swallow me whole? And if we part,
are we severed? Is a limb a body
severed too? Am I body become a you
become a limb? Will I wake some day
soon to find that once again I am arms,
that I am legs and sides and shins?
Will I be the same body? Will we?

I feel the raw end of me, perfect
for attachment, prone to collecting
cat hair, grit, and dust. What I've lost
is where I came from. There is no speed,
only velocity. No travel, just a nauseous
moment when I learned I've been a top,
an in-place rushing. And not one of you
was as much a person as potential,
as speed. A hard hip against the table.

SEX PEOPLE

Sometimes I wonder what the sexy people do,
where do they go when they aren't being sex
people? When the lubricant is gone, the rug frays
too far. Who stands from the pile to find their keys,
to find the nearest weaver? I thought I was a sex
person. I'm not. I was just confused. I thought
since one fucks so closely, it must make us sort
of close. But you can fuck anyone. You really can.
It doesn't seem like it, but you can pretty much
sex an idea these days, a ghost. Don't limit yourself
is all I'm saying. That, and also that I was wrong.
You have to do it if she doesn't feel pretty,
or she really likes you, like a lot. If he drove you
and your friends all the way home from school,
if he didn't tell the other teachers about the porn,
if she's drunk and puts your hand up her skirt.
You know, I met one, a real sex man. He fucked
anything. They're everywhere now. You could fill
a truck with them. Two trucks. I can't even get a seat
on the bus to work. There are orgies in the aisles.

GOSLING

Do you remember when you and Ryan kept coming
up for all the same roles? Just after you shaved your
head and had that madness. You'd never been more.
Your head was so round. I'll never be beautiful like that,
never be pretty. Small, I know, but it would have been
neat to try. Do you think we'd be different if you had
made it to the *Drive* audition? I'd ask, *Are you crazy?*
Wait, am I? and you'd work on your stare, that practiced
Hey kid, you want a toothpick? You would have rocked
the jacket and gloves, and you could get the hang
of the action stuff. It's mostly stunt people anyway.
But instead of your best *My hands are a little dirty*,
you spent the night in the ward, and Ryan got the part.
I know they wouldn't have paid you what he got paid,
but it maybe would have been enough for us to talk.

RANDOMIZER

In this one, I go to school in Alberta and you work at the hospital as an ultrasound tech. For a while, I thought I'd find you shattering forth from the rabbit's neck, crystal bursting from anywhere I twist too hard. I saw a sculpture once, these hares with their necks broken and a line of white crystals jutting from their wounds. I know the artist must have believed what I believed, in the stars beneath our skin, the secret, the glitch, and they learned what I am learning, that there is no secret to life. In this one, you hunt moose with your father in northern Manitoba, and I'm one of the pregnancies you lost. Since his eyes started going, you shoot and he cuts, but his knife now strays toward the meat. Departing, you look back, you confuse proximity for fluency, expect to read the blood on the snow, but come up short. In this one, you're the stranger in the hospital bed next to me. I come back to visit you. I'm learning to bake bread. It's how I got better, I say. But you smelled it on me from the hallway. You've seen secrets up close.

THE WORST

I went on a date the other night. She was much cooler than me, but I found her online, saw that her mother died of breast cancer, and she had written a few comments under her initials on the memorial page. There were errors in her grammar. I told her about how I don't participate in work activities, but maybe I'd put a team together for this breast cancer run. I stared at the table. *It's an important cause to me*, I said. She said she liked having sex with me. I could tell she was shocked at how much I sweat. The Adderall, probably. I told her that, now, I'm on the edge of a depression, that now, I have to focus on just being okay, right now. She's big on mental health. I still have the pictures she sent. Tame, but they help me stand a little better if I bring them up in the stall of a public washroom or on the way to a party, help me talk to the people if that's what I'm doing. Really, I told her, I don't participate at work, but I do like that we fundraise, I donate sometimes. I told her you had a mastectomy and so did your sister(s). And I am on the edge of it. I do need to focus on my shit. I told her you came home laughing afterward, popping your dentures in and out. I never told her what I said. I don't think we'll talk again — not any of us.

WE FORGET WE ARE

The same scream of awareness, the sun dipping
itself into a body for a billionth of a second.
We are the spinning light, so thin and quick
you can't even tell we're not here anymore.
What is me and you, is what is now. If it spins
fast enough, an LED can look like anything,
like it's everywhere it's ever been. My son
asks me if it's the bulb or the electricity we
see when we look at the light, but I am alone,
and I'm afraid I am the filament. I worry too
that we are all the electricity, dipping in
and out of the bulbs so quick and bright we
think we're bodies. I tell him I'm worried.
My son holds me on the couch, promises
I won't be alone forever. But tomorrow
is a threadbare blanket, and I am cold today.

A MAGIC

For ending other people's calls. For making a child's
skin turn hard as stone. To make the liver work like
it's Adderalled for the very first time. Magic to make
your houseplants touch your legs at night. A spell
to return to any city. To forget how small you are!
A magic to grow taller, stand better, sit well. A spell
to make them disappear, another to bring them back.
To regrow, pregrow hair. Magic for free electrolysis,
for preheating the oven, for never changing your mind.
A song that kills who you should kill. A magic for undoing.
A glyph to stop the carousel and one to spin forever.

FATHER FLIRTING

I once wrote a short story about my father flirting, saying *darling* to
every woman we met, holding my head between himself and the
hairdresser, showing her the baby fuzz on the back of my neck,
guiding her fingers to the soft hairs. In the subdivision, we lived next
to Sandy, whom you hated. The single mom, California tan and hair.
I remember playing Candyland with her daughter, younger than me,
and watching Sandy change with her back to me in the bedroom,
the jokes you'd make about her and Dad, a little bit of jealousy you
knew wasn't real. The air between my father and the hairdresser
cutting my hair was thinner than anywhere else on earth. I didn't
know you could make a mountain grow like that. I didn't know that
sometimes, when you feel the air sucked out of a room, it means
it's time to run.

DEATH, MY CANADIAN GIRLFRIEND

I don't know how to say to a friend about his dead sister
that I'm sorry. That it must feel like a hole in the world,
like all his life is a lake and some fool has pulled the plug.
He'd make fists. I know it. I'm sorry, I'd say. I didn't know her,
but if she was like him, and she would be, she was beautiful.
Her inside larger than her out. If she was like their father,
she was a gateway, deep and endless, a body of holding.
The lost friend whose brother died, the brother who taught
me French, then how to escape a leghold in front of the class.
I'd tell her I didn't understand, but I'd do my best to hold
that glimmer of him for her, to travel with it. I tell it to my
bowl until the ice cream melts. The bowl whispers back,
You're nothing to me. I try a joke, but the bowl is deadpan.
I drip vanilla from the spoon. Our Sundays remain sour.

OTTERING

In my shorts on the couch, I've been trying
to stack these little stones on my belly.
I balance them on my abdomen and consider
people I no longer see. Building makes
me nervous. Did you know that Lego wants
its name to be un-nounable? But we don't
choose our names, Lego. I used to smash kids'
toys hoping to be stopped. Ruining things is easy
if you put your shoulder to it. Dave told me once
about looking at his first kid, and at the knife,
and his child, the knife. He's been ecstatic
cince day one. We always knew he'd have a son.
He once bought locks for the eyewash in case
someone poisoned the water, maxed his credit
on D2 rune trading. During every blink he saw
his fortune, the next big win. *The stones are not
what you think*, I'd say. *I'm hoping for a boy.*

MY THERAPIST ASKS ME HOW I THINK THE BOYS FROM SCHOOL ARE DOING

You'd be surprised I have a therapist — what with
how I ran away from the psychiatrist and Al-Anon
meetings. Do you know though? Are you in touch
with any of the mothers? Were those boys stricken
silent too? Did they sprout from our bed of noise
into mute protagonists? Did you have a fever during
character creation? Do the boys know to love one
another? Once, at a show, a friend read aloud each
way there is to make a boy. It's a dream we share:
a perfect boy. Do you think — if you did it just right,
not a hair in the mould — you could make one that
would never lose his voice? One that conjured words
right into adulthood. Could you make one where if he
dies, he'll have friends to carry him? Will his therapist
find someone quickly for nine on Thursdays? Someone
who kept in touch? Do you think that you could make
my therapist a boy who knows how the other boys are
doing? One who stuck with them, who kissed the tops
of their heads after breakups, and wrote their finals
when their fathers were in the hospital. If I got a manual,
do you think you could make a boy for my girlfriend?
One who makes fires from flint, braids her hair in new
and interesting ways. Make me a boy for the woman
I love. A safe boy. A classic boy. A blonde. Your curls.

KNOWING

There are two kinds of knowing: the one that knows
above, like a hawk that sees nothing of the meadow,
knows, a mile out, the shake of heartbeats under fur;
and the prey, who knows below, knows each pebble
stepped on, each flower hid behind or eaten. And there
is a third kind of knowing, in the bones, in how hands
can interlock the first time they meet. I once thought
the body had a quiet knowing. There are maybe six.
The separate becoming together. A friend who makes
space for your wide left turns, who stands on the side
with your good eye. It's the same knowing. Leave the
guild, swap factions, server transfer, but you'll end up
in the same place, unless you change the way you raid.
I wish I'd known that protecting is not the same as making
safe, that hating yourself is not the same as changing.

GLOSSARY

ROGUELIKE comes from *Rogue*, a computer game released in 1980 characterized by its procedurally generated levels, turn-based combat/exploration, and permanent character death. A roguelike is a subgenre of role-playing game which shares some of these characteristics.

GRINDING typically refers to periods in gameplay when a player repeats specific tasks for a long stretch of time in order to receive rewards such as increased power relative to enemies, a specific item/ability, or simply a cosmetic marker indicating that the player has accomplished a time-consuming feat.

KONAMI CODE is a famous cheat code originally used in Konami games to unlock developer options, gameplay advantages, or cosmetic changes. In modern games and pop culture, it usually functions as an in-joke or Easter egg. The code: up, up, down, down, left, right, left, right, B, A.

A HEATMAP is a top-down view of a game environment typically used in shooter games to indicate places where player deaths or kills occur. In a multiplayer game, a heatmap can be used to detect imbalances in the layout of the game map, which might lend one team or position an advantage.

NPC stands for *non-player character*, a character in a role-playing game who is not directly controlled by any of the players.

RIP, pronounced like "rip," is a casual repurposing of *R.I.P.* usually used in less serious circumstances than the original or simply to express disappointment. "I stepped in vomit. Rip my pants."

A GHOST CAR, most often seen in racing games, is an in-game representation of a previous attempt at the track. Depending on the game, a ghost car may represent many things, from the best race stored on your local machine to your most recent attempt at the track — or even the previous performance of an unknown player online.

VANISH/X-ZONE is a spell combination in *Final Fantasy VI* that trivialized almost all combat by allowing the player to end a fight very quickly and using few resources. As this spell effect wasn't intended, using this combination at the wrong time could effectively make the game incompletable.

RAID refers to specific high-difficulty content taking place near the end of a game. A raid usually requires exceptional teamwork and communication from a large number of accomplished/powerful players.

ACKNOWLEDGEMENTS

This book was made possible through generous financial support from the Canada Council for the Arts and the Ontario Arts Council.

I couldn't have written the collection without Kevin Connolly, a wildly insightful editor and an endlessly supportive friend.

I'm also very grateful to Gil Adamson for her stellar copyediting and gaming knowledge.

The entire Anansi team deserves praise and gratitude, and I'm especially thankful to Maria Golikova, who responds to each of my panicked emails with calm professionalism.

So much is owed to Kellie, Marki, Stephanie, Meg, Pavan, and Gio for their friendship, support, and kindness.

I have been fortunate to benefit from the hard work, experience, and generosity of fellow poets Robin Richardson, Bardia Sinaee, Jeff Latosik, Braydon Beaulieu, Jacob McArthur Mooney, and the many others who offered comments and thoughtful criticism online, over dinner, and in PlayStation party chats.

In "Severance," the line "Let me out let me out this is not a dance" is from the eighteenth episode of *Rick and Morty*.

Imagery from "Randomizer" is inspired by Philippa Jones's *Perpetual* at the Confederation Centre for the Arts.

MATHEW HENDERSON's first book, *The Lease*, was a finalist for both the Trillium Book Award for Poetry and the Gerald Lampert Memorial Award. Henderson earned an M.F.A. from the University of Guelph and has had poems published in *The Walrus*, *Brick*, *Maisonneuve*, and *Best Canadian Poetry*.